The Poetry of Bliss Carman

Volume VI - By the Aurelian Wall & Other Elegies

William Bliss Carman was born in Fredericton, in New Brunswick on April 15th 1861. He was educated at Fredericton Collegiate School before moving to the University of New Brunswick, obtaining his B.A. there in 1881. As is common with so many writers his first published piece was for the University magazine and for Carman that was in 1879.

After several years editing various magazines and periodicals Carman first published a poetry volume in 1893 with Low Tide on Grand Pré. There was no Canadian company prepared to publish and when an American company did so it went bankrupt.

The following year was decidedly better. His partnership with the American poet Richard Hovey had given birth to Songs of Vagabondia. It was an immediate success.

That success prompted the Boston firm, Stone & Kimball, to reissue Low Tide on Grand Pré and to hire Carman as the editor of its literary journal, The Chapbook.

Carman brought out, in 1895, Behind the Arras, a somewhat more serious and philosophical work centered on the premise of a long meditation, using the speaker's house and its many rooms, as a symbol of life and the choices to be made.

In 1896 Carman met Mrs Mary Perry King, who rapidly became patron, adviser and sometime lover. She also became his writing collaborator on two verse dramas.

In 1897 Carman published Ballad of Lost Haven, and in 1898, By the Aurelian Wall, the title poem itself was an elegy to John Keats and the book was a collection of formal elegies.

As the century turned Carman was hard at work on a five-volume set of poetry "Pans Pipes". The excellence of a number of these poems did much to install Carman as the most noted of Canadian Poets and eventually their own Poet Laureate.

In 1912 the final work in the Vagabondia series was published. Richard Hovey had died in 1900 and so this last work was purely Carman's. It has a distinct elegiac tone as if remembering the past works themselves.

On October 28th, 1921 Carman was honored by the newly-formed Canadian Authors' Association where he was crowned Canada's Poet Laureate with a wreath of maple leaves.

William Bliss Carman died of a brain hemorrhage at the age of 68 in New Canaan on the 8th June, 1929.

Index of Contents

BY THE AURELIAN WALL

In Memory of John Keats

By the Aurelian Wall,
Where the long shadows of the centuries fall
From Caius Cestius' tomb,
A weary mortal seeking rest found room
For quiet burial,

Leaving among his friends
A book of lyrics.
Such untold amends
A traveller might make
In a strange country, bidden to partake
Before he farther wends;

Who shyly should bestow
The foreign reed-flute they had seen him blow
And finger cunningly,
On one of the dark children standing by,
Then lift his cloak and go.

The years pass. And the child
Thoughtful beyond his fellows, grave and mild,
Treasures the rough-made toy,

Until one day he blows it for clear joy,
And wakes the music wild.

His fondness makes it seem
A thing first fashioned in delirious dream,
Some god had cut and tried,
And filled with yearning passion, and cast aside
On some far woodland stream,—

After long years to be
Found by the stranger and brought over sea,
A marvel and delight
To ease the noon and pierce the dark blue night,
For children such as he.

He learns the silver strain
Wherewith the ghostly houses of gray rain
And lonely valleys ring,
When the untroubled whitethroats make the spring
A world without a stain;

Then on his river reed,
With strange and unsuspected notes that plead
Of their own wild accord
For utterances no bird's throat could afford,
Lifts it to human need.

His comrades leave their play,
When calling and compelling far away
By river-slope and hill,
He pipes their wayward footsteps where he will,
All the long lovely day.

Even his elders come.
"Surely the child is elvish," murmur some,
And shake the knowing head;
"Give us the good old simple things instead,
Our fathers used to hum."

Others at the open door
Smile when they hear what they have hearkened for
These many summers now,
Believing they should live to learn somehow
Things never known before.

But he can only tell
How the flute's whisper lures him with a spell,
Yet always just eludes

The lost perfection over which he broods;
And how he loves it well.

Till all the country-side,
Familiar with his piping far and wide,
Has taken for its own
That weird enchantment down the evening blown,—
Its glory and its pride.

And so his splendid name,
Who left the book of lyrics and small fame
Among his fellows then,
Spreads through the world like autumn—who knows when?—
Till all the hillsides flame.

Grand Pré and Margaree
Hear it upbruited from the unresting sea;
And the small Gaspareau,
Whose yellow leaves repeat it, seems to know
A new felicity.

Even the shadows tall,
Walking at sundown through the plain, recall
A mound the grasses keep,
Where once a mortal came and found long sleep
By the Aurelian Wall.

THE WHITE GULL

For the Centenary of the Birth of Shelley

I

Up by the idling reef-set bell
The tide comes in;
And to the idle heart to-day
The wind has many things to say;
The sea has many a tale to tell
His younger kin.

For we are his, bone of his bone,
Breath of his breath;
The doom tides sway us at their will;
The sky of being rounds us still;
And over us at last is blown
The wind of death.

II

A hundred years ago to-day
There came a soul,
A pilgrim of the perilous light,
Treading the spheral paths of night,
On whom the word and vision lay
With dread control.

Now the pale Summer lingers near,
And talks to me
Of all her wayward journeyings,
And the old, sweet, forgotten things
She loved and lost and dreamed of here
By the blue sea.

The great cloud-navies, one by one,
Bend sails and fill
From ports below the round sea-verge;
I watch them gather and emerge,
And steer for havens of the sun
Beyond the hill.

The gray sea-horses troop and roam;
The shadows fly
Along the wind-floor at their heels;
And where the golden daylight wheels,
A white gull searches the blue dome
With keening cry.

And something, Shelley, like thy fame
Dares the wide morn
In that sea-rover's glimmering flight,
As if the Northland and the night
Should hear thy splendid valiant name
Put scorn to scorn.

III

Thou heart of all the hearts of men,
Tameless and free,
And vague as that marsh-wandering fire,
Leading the world's outworn desire
A night march down this ghostly fen
From sea to sea!

Through this divided camp of dream
Thy feet have passed,
As one who should set hand to rouse
His comrades from their heavy drowse;
For only their own deeds redeem
God's sons at last.

But the dim world will dream and sleep
Beneath thy hand,
As poppies in the windy morn,
Or valleys where the standing corn
Whispers when One goes forth to reap
The weary land.

O captain of the rebel host,
Lead forth and far!
Thy toiling troopers of the night
Press on the unavailing fight;
The sombre field is not yet lost,
With thee for star.

Thy lips have set the hail and haste
Of clarions free
To bugle down the wintry verge
Of time forever, where the surge
Thunders and crumbles on a waste
And open sea.

IV

Did the cold Norns who pattern life
With haste and rest
Take thought to cheer their pilgrims on
Through trackless twilights vast and wan,
Across the failure and the strife,
From quest to quest,—

Set their last kiss upon thy face,
And let thee go
To tell the haunted whisperings
Of unimaginable things,
Which plague thy fellows with a trace
They cannot know?

So they might fashion and send forth
Their house of doom,

Through the pale splendor of the night,
In vibrant, hurled, impetuous flight,
A resonant meteor of the North
From gloom to gloom.

V

I think thou must have wandered far
With Spring for guide,
And heard the shy-born forest flowers
Talk to the wind among the showers,
Through sudden doorways left ajar
When the wind sighed;

Thou must have heard the marching sweep
Of blown white rain
Go volleying up the icy kills,—
And watched with Summer when the hills
Muttered of freedom in their sleep
And slept again.

Surely thou wert a lonely one,
Gentle and wild;
And the round sun delayed for thee
In the red moorlands by the sea,
When Tyrian Autumn lured thee on,
A wistful child,

To rove the tranquil, vacant year,
From dale to dale;
And the great Mother took thy face
Between her hands for one long gaze,
And bade thee follow without fear
The endless trail.

And thy clear spirit, half forlorn,
Seeking its own,
Dwelt with the nomad tents of rain,
Marched with the gold-red ranks of grain,
Or ranged the frontiers of the morn,
And was alone.

VI

One brief perturbed and glorious day!
How couldst thou learn

The quiet of the forest sun,
Where the dark, whispering rivers run
The journey that hath no delay
And no return?

And yet within thee flamed and sang
The dauntless heart,
Knowing all passion and the pain
On man's imperious disdain,
Since God's great part in thee gave pang
To earth's frail part.

It held the voices of the hills
Deep in its core;
The wandering shadows of the sea
Called to it,—would not let it be;
The harvest of those barren rills
Was in its store.

Thine was a love that strives and calls
Outcast from home,
Burning to free the soul of man
With some new life. How strange, a ban
Should set thy sleep beneath the walls
Of changeless Rome!

VII

More soft, I deem, from spring to spring,
Thy sleep would be
Where this far western headland lies
With its imperial azure skies,
Under thee hearing beat and swing
The eternal sea.

Where all the livelong brooding day
And all night long,
The far sea-journeying wind should come
Down to the doorway of thy home,
To lure thee ever the old way
With the old song.

But the dim forest would so house
Thy heart so dear,
Even the low surf of the rain,
Where ghostly centuries complain,
Might beat against thy door and rouse

No heartache here.

For here the thrushes, calm, supreme,
Forever reign,
Whose gloriously kingly golden throats
Regather their forgotten notes
In keys where lurk no ruin of dream,
No tinge of pain.

And here the ruthless noisy sea,
With the tide's will,
The strong gray wrestler, should in vain
Put forth his hand on thee again—
Lift up his voice and call to thee,
And thou be still.

For thou hast overcome at last;
And fate and fear
And strife and rumor now no more
Vex thee by any wind-vexed shore,
Down the strewn ways thy feet have passed
Far, far from here.

VIII

Up by the idling, idling bell
The tide comes in;
And to the restless heart to-day
The wind has many things to say;
The sea has many a tale to tell
His younger kin.

The gray sea-horses troop and roam;
The shadows fly
Along the wind-floor at their heels;
And where the golden daylight wheels,
A white gull searches the blue dome
With keening cry.

THE COUNTRY OF HAR

For the Centenary of Blake's "Songs of Innocence"

Once a hundred years ago
There was a light in London town,

For an angel of the snow
Walked her street sides up and down.

As a visionary boy
He put forth his hand to smite
Songs of innocence and joy
From the crying chords of night,
Like a muttering of thunder
Heard beneath the polar star;
For his soul was all a-wonder
At the calling vales of Har.

He, a traveller by day
And a pilgrim of the sun,
Took his uncompanioned way
Where the journey is not done.

Where no mortal might aspire
His clear heart was set to climb,
To the uplands of desire
And the river wells of time.

Home he wandered to the valley
Where the springs of morning are,
And the sea-bright cohorts rally
On the twilit plains of Har.

There he found the Book of Thel
In the lily-garth of bliss,
Fashioned, how no man can tell,
As a white windflower is:

Like the lulling of a sigh
Uttered in the trembling grass,
When a shower is gone by,
And the sweeping shadows pass,—

Through the hyacinthine weather,
Wheel them down without a jar,—
Heaving all the dappled heather
In the streaming vales of Har.

There was manna in the rain;
And above the rills, a voice:
"Son of mine, dost thou complain?
I will make thee to rejoice.

"Thou shalt be a child to men,

With confusion on thy speech;
And the worlds within thy ken
Shall not lie within thy reach.

"But the rainbirds shall discover,
And the daffodils unbar,
Quiet waters for their lover
On the shining plains of Har.

"April rain and iron frost
Shall make flowers to thy hand;
Every field thy feet have crossed
Shall revive from death's command.

"Hunting with a leash of wind
Through the corners of the earth,
Take the hounds of Spring to find
The forgotten trails of mirth;

"For the lone child-heart is dying
Of a love no time can mar,
Hearing not a voice replying
From the gladder vales of Har.

"Flame thy heart forth! Yet, no haste:
Have not I prepared for thee
The king's chambers of the East
And the wind halls of the sea?

"Be a gospeller of things
Nowhere written through the wild,
With that gloaming call of Spring's,
When old secrets haunt the child.

"Let the bugler of my going
Wake no clarion of war;
For the paper reeds are blowing
On the river plains of Har."

Centuries of soiled renown
To the roaring dark have gone:
There is woe in London town,
And a crying for the dawn.

April frost and iron rain
Ripen the dead fruit of lust,
And the sons of God remain
The dream children of the dust,

For their heart hath in derision,
And their jeers have mocked afar,
The delirium of vision
From the holy vales of Har.

Once in Autumn came a dream;
The white Herald of the North,
Faring West to ford my stream,
Passed my lodge and bade me forth;

Glad I rose and went with him,
With my shoulder in his hand;
The auroral world grew dim,
And the idle harvest land.

Then I saw the warder lifting
From its berg the Northern bar,
And eternal snows were drifting
On the wind-bleak plains of Har.

"Listen humbly," said my guide.
"I am drear, for I am death,"
Whispered Snow; but Wind replied,
"I outlive thee by a breath,

I am Time." And then I heard,
Dearer than all wells of dew,
One gray golden-shafted bird
Hail the uplands; so I knew

Spring, the angel of our sorrow,
Tarrying so seeming far,
Should return with some long morrow
In the calling vales of Har.

TO RICHARD LOVELACE

Ah, Lovelace, what desires have sway
In the white shadow of your heart,
Which no more measures day by day,
Nor sets the years apart?

How many seasons for your sake
Have taught men over, age by age,
"Stone walls do not a prison make,

Nor iron bars a cage!"—

Since that first April when you fared
Into the Gatehouse, well content,
Caring for nothing so you cared
For honor and for Kent.

How many, since the April rain
Beat drear and blossomless and hoar
Through London, when you left Shoe Lane,
A-marching to no war!

Till now, with April on the sea,
And sunshine in the woven year,
The rain-winds loose from reverie
A lyric and a cheer.

A SEAMARK

A Threnody for Robert Louis Stevenson

Cold, the dull cold! What ails the sun,
And takes the heart out of the day?
What makes the morning look so mean,
The Common so forlorn and gray?

The wintry city's granite heart
Beats on in iron mockery,
And like the roaming mountain rains,
I hear the thresh of feet go by.

It is the lonely human surf
Surging through alleys chill with grime,
The muttering churning ceaseless floe
Adrift out of the North of time.

Fades, it all fades! I only see
The poster with its reds and blues
Bidding the heart stand still to take
Its desolating stab of news.

That intimate and magic name:
"Dead in Samoa." ... Cry your cries,
O city of the golden dome,
Under the gray Atlantic skies!

But I have wander-biddings now.
Far down the latitudes of sun,
An island mountain of the sea,
Piercing the green and rosy zone,

Goes up into the wondrous day.
And there the brown-limbed island men
Are bearing up for burial,
Within the sun's departing ken,

The master of the roving kind.
And there where time will set no mark
For his irrevocable rest,
Under the spacious melting dark,

With all the nomad tented stars
About him, they have laid him down
Above the crumbling of the sea,
Beyond the turmoil of renown.

O all you hearts about the world
In whom the truant gipsy blood,
Under the frost of this pale time,
Sleeps like the daring sap and flood

That dream of April and reprieve!
You whom the haunted vision drives,
Incredulous of home and ease,
Perfection's lovers all your lives!

You whom the wander-spirit loves
To lead by some forgotten clue
Forever vanishing beyond
Horizon brinks forever new;

The road, unmarked, ordained, whereby
Your brothers of the field and air
Before you, faithful, blind and glad,
Emerged from chaos pair by pair;

The road whereby you too must come,
In the unvexed and fabled years
Into the country of your dream,
With all your knowledge in arrears!

You, who can never quite forget
Your glimpse of Beauty as she passed,
The well-head where her knee was pressed,

The dew wherein her foot was cast;

O you who bid the paint and clay
Be glorious when you are dead,
And fit the plangent words in rhyme
Where the dark secret lurks unsaid;

You brethren of the light-heart guild,
The mystic fellowcraft of joy,
Who tarry for the news of truth,
And listen for some vast ahoy

Blown in from sea, who crowd the wharves
With eager eyes that wait the ship
Whose foreign tongue may fill the world
With wondrous tales from lip to lip;

Our restless loved adventurer,
On secret orders come to him,
Has slipped his cable, cleared the reef,
And melted on the white sea-rim.

O granite hills, go down in blue!
And like green clouds in opal calms,
You anchored islands of the main,
Float up your loom of feathery palms!

For deep within your dales, where lies
A valiant earthling stark and dumb,
This savage undiscerning heart
Is with the silent chiefs who come

To mourn their kin and bear him gifts,—
Who kiss his hand, and take their place,
This last night he receives his friends,
The journey-wonder on his face.

He "was not born for age." Ah no,
For everlasting youth is his!
Part of the lyric of the earth
With spring and leaf and blade he is.

'Twill nevermore be April now
But there will lurk a thought of him
At the street corners, gay with flowers
From rainy valleys purple-dim.

O chiefs, you do not mourn alone!

In that stern North where mystery broods,
Our mother grief has many sons
Bred in those iron solitudes.

It does not help them, to have laid
Their coil of lightning under seas;
They are as impotent as you
To mend the loosened wrists and knees.

And yet how many a harvest night,
When the great luminous meteors flare
Along the trenches of the dusk,
The men who dwell beneath the Bear,

Seeing those vagrants of the sky
Float through the deep beyond their hark,
Like Arabs through the wastes of air,—
A flash, a dream, from dark to dark,—

Must feel the solemn large surmise:
By a dim vast and perilous way
We sweep through undetermined time,
Illumining this quench of clay,

A moment staunched, then forth again.
Ah, not alone you climb the steep
To set your loving burden down
Against the mighty knees of sleep.

With you we hold the sombre faith
Where creeds are sown like rain at sea;
And leave the loveliest child of earth
To slumber where he longed to be.

His fathers lit the dangerous coast
To steer the daring merchant home;
His courage lights the dark'ning port
Where every sea-worn sail must come.

And since he was the type of all
That strain in us which still must fare,
The fleeting migrant of a day,
Heart-high, outbound for otherwhere,

Now therefore, where the passing ships
Hang on the edges of the noon,
And Northern liners trail their smoke
Across the rising yellow moon,

Bound for his home, with shuddering screw
That beats its strength out into speed,
Until the pacing watch descries
On the sea-line a scarlet seed

Smolder and kindle and set fire
To the dark selvedge of the night,
The deep blue tapestry of stars,
Then sheet the dome in pearly light,

There in perpetual tides of day,
Where men may praise him and deplore,
The place of his lone grave shall be
A seamark set forevermore,

High on a peak adrift with mist,
And round whose bases, far beneath
The snow-white wheeling tropic birds,
The emerald dragon breaks his teeth.

THE WORD OF THE WATER

For the Unveiling of the Stevenson Fountain in San Francisco

God made me simple from the first,
And good to quench your body's thirst.
Think you he has no ministers
To glad that wayworn soul of yours?

Here by the thronging Golden Gate
For thousands and for you I wait,
Seeing adventurous sails unfurled
For the four corners of the world.

Here passed one day, nor came again,
A prince among the tribes of men.
(For man, like me, is from his birth
A vagabond upon this earth.)

Be thankful, friend, as you pass on,
And pray for Louis Stevenson,
That by whatever trail he fare
He be refreshed in God's great care!

This is the white winter day of his burial.
Time has set here of his toiling the span
Earthward, naught else. Cheer him out through the portal,
Heart-beat of Boston, our utmost in man!

Out in the broad open sun be his funeral,
Under the blue for the city to see.
Over the grieving crowd mourn for him, bugle!
Churches are narrow to hold such as he.

Here on the steps of the temple he builded,
Rest him a space, while the great city square
Throngs with his people, his thousands, his mourners;
Tears for his peace and a multitude's prayer.

How comes it, think you, the town's traffic pauses
Thus at high noon? Can we wealthmongers grieve?
Here in the sad surprise greatest America
Shows for a moment her heart on her sleeve.

She who is said to give life-blood for silver,
Proves, without show, she sets higher than gold
Just the straight manhood, clean, gentle, and fearless,
Made in God's likeness once more as of old.

Once more the crude makeshift law overproven,—
Soul pent from sin will seek God in despite;
Once more the gladder way wins revelation,—
Soul bent on God forgets evil outright.

Once more the seraph voice sounding to beauty,
Once more the trumpet tongue bidding, no fear!
Once more the new, purer plan's vindication,—
Man be God's forecast, and Heaven is here.

Bear him to burial, Harvard, thy hero!
Not on thy shoulders alone is he borne;
They of the burden go forth on the morrow,
Heavy and slow, through a world left forlorn.

No grief for him, for ourselves the lamenting;
What giant arm to stay courage up now?
March we a thousand file up to the City,
Fellow with fellow linked, he taught us how!

Never dismayed at the dark nor the distance!
Never deployed for the steep nor the storm!
Hear him say, "Hold fast, the night wears to morning!
This God of promise is God to perform."

Up with thee, heart of fear, high as the heaven!
Thou hast known one wore this life without stain.
What if for thee and me,—street, Yard, or Common,—
Such a white captain appear not again!

Fight on alone! Let the faltering spirit
Within thee recall how he carried a host,
Rearward and van, as Wind shoulders a dust-heap;
One Way till strife be done, strive each his most.

Take the last vesture of beauty upon thee,
Thou doubting world; and with not an eye dim
Say, when they ask if thou knowest a Saviour,
"Brooks was His brother, and we have known him."

JOHN ELIOT BOWEN

Here at the desk where once you sat,
Who wander now with poets dead
And summers gone, afield so far,
There sits a stranger in your stead.

Here day by day men come who knew
Your steadfast ways and loved you well;
And every comer with regret
Has some new thing of praise to tell.

The poet old, whose lyric heart
Is fresh as dew and bright as flame,
Longs for "his boy," and finds you not,
And goes the wistful way he came.

Here where you toiled without reproach,
Builded and loved and dreamed and planned,
At every door, on every page,
Lurks the tradition of your hand.

And if to you, like reverie,
There comes a thought of how they fare
Whose footsteps go the round you went
Of noisy street and narrow stair,

Know they have learned a new desire,
Which puts unfaith and faltering by;
And triumph fills their dream because
One life was leal, one hope was high.

HENRY GEORGE

We are only common people,
And he was a man like us.
But he loved his fellows before himself;
And he died for me and you,
To redeem the world anew
From cruelty and greed—
For love the only creed,
For honor the only law.

There once was a man of the people,
A man like you and me,
Who worked for his daily bread,
And he loved his fellows before himself.
But he died at the hands of the throng
To redeem the world from wrong,
And we call him the Son of God,
Because of the love he had.

And there was a man of the people,
Who sat in the people's chair,
And bade the slaves go free;
For he loved his fellows before himself.
They took his life; but his word
They could not take. It was heard
Over the beautiful earth,
A thunder and whisper of love.

And there is no other way,
Since man of woman was born,
Than the way of the rebels and saints,
With loving and labor vast,
To redeem the world at last
From cruelty and greed;
For love is the only creed,
And honor the only law.

ILICET

Friends, let him rest
In midnight now.
Desire has gone
On the weary quest
With aching brow;
Until the dawn,
Friends, let him rest.

With a boy's desire
He set the cup
To his lips to drink;
The ruddy fire
Was lifted up
At day's cool brink,
With a boy's desire.

The heart of a boy!
He tasted life,
And the bitter sting
Of sorrow in joy,
Failure in strife,
Was pain to wring
The heart of a boy.

In a childish whim,
He spilled the wine
Upon the floor,—
In beads on the brim
Was a glitter of brine,—
Then, out at the door
In a childish whim!

Out of the storm,
In the flickering light,
A broken glass
Lies on our warm
Hearthstone to-night,
While shadows pass
Out of the storm.

Friends, let him rest
In midnight now.
Desire has gone
On the weary quest
With aching brow:
Until the dawn,

Friends, let him rest.

In sorrow and shame
For the craven heart,
In manhood's breast
With valor's name,
Let him depart
Unto his rest
In sorrow and shame.

In after years
God, who bestows
Or withholds the valor,
Shall wipe all tears—
Haply, who knows?—
From his face's pallor
In after years.

He could not learn
To fight with his peers
In sturdier fashion;
Let him return
Through the night with tears,
Stung with the passion
He could not learn.

All-bountiful, calm,
Where the great stars burn,
And the spring bloom smothers
The night with balm,
Let him return
To the silent Mother's
All-bountiful calm.

Friends, let him rest
In midnight now.
Desire has gone
On the weary quest
With aching brow:
Until the dawn,
Friends, let him rest.

TO RAPHAEL

Master of adored Madonnas,
What is this men say of thee?

Thou wert something less than honor's
Most exact epitome?

Yes, they say you loved too many,
Loved too often, loved too well.
Just as if there could be any
Over-loving, Raphael!

Was it, "Sir, and how came this tress,
Long and raven? Mine are gold!"
You should have made Art your mistress,
Lived an anchorite and old!

Ah, no doubt these dear good people
On familiar terms with God,
Could devise a parish steeple
Built to heaven without a hod.

You and Solomon and Cæsar
Were three fellows of a kind;
Not a woman but to please her
You would leave your soul behind.

Those dead women with their beauty,
How they must have loved you well,—
Dared to make desire a duty,
With the heretics in hell!

And your brother, that Catullus,
What a plight he must be in,
If those silver songs that lull us
Were result of mortal sin!

If the artist were ungodly,
Prurient of mind and heart,
I must think they argue oddly
Who make shrines before his art.

Not the meanest aspiration
Ever sprung from soul depraved
Into art, but art's elation
Was the sanctity it craved.

Oh, no doubt you had your troubles,
Devils blue that blanched your hope.
I dare say your fancy's bubbles,
Breaking, had a taste of soap.

Did your lady-loves undo you
In some mediæval way?
Ah, my Raphael, here's to you!
It is much the same to-day.

Did their tantalizing laughter
Make your wisdom overbold?
Were you fire at first; and after,
Did their kisses leave you cold?

Did some fine perfidious Nancy,
With the roses in her hair,
Play the marsh-fire to your fancy
Over quagmires of despair?

My poor boy, were there more flowers
In your Florence and your Rome,
Wasting through the gorgeous hours,
Than your two hands could bring home?

Be content; you have your glory;
Life was full and sleep is well.
What the end is of the story,
There's no paragraph to tell.

TO P. V.

So they would raise your monument,
Old vagabond of lovely earth?
Another answer without words
To Humdrum's, "What are poets worth?"

Not much we gave you when alive,
Whom now we lavishly deplore,—
A little bread, a little wine,
A little caporal—no more.

Here in our lodging of a day
You roistered till we were appalled;
Departing, in your room we found
A string of golden verses scrawled.

The princely manor-house of art,
A vagrant artist entertains;
And when he gets him to the road,
Behold, a princely gift remains.

Abashed, we set your name above
The purse-full patrons of our board;
Remind newcomers with a nudge,
"Verlaine took once what we afford!"

The gardens of the Luxembourg,
Spreading beneath the brilliant sun,
Shall be your haunt of leisure now
When all your wander years are done.

There you shall stand, the very mien
You wore in Paris streets of old,
And ponder what a thing is life,
Or watch the chestnut blooms unfold.

There you will find, I dare surmise,
Another tolerance than ours,
The loving-kindness of the grass,
The tender patience of the flowers.

And every year, when May returns
To bring the golden age again,
And hope comes back with poetry
In your loved land across the Seine,

Some youth will come with foreign speech,
Bearing his dream from over sea,
A lover of your flawless craft,
Apprenticed to your poverty.

He will be mute before you there,
And mark those lineaments which tell
What stormy unrelenting fate
Had one who served his art so well.

And there be yours, the livelong day,
Beyond the mordant reach of pain,
The little gospel of the leaves,
The Nunc dimittis of the rain!

A NORSE CHILD'S REQUIEM

Sleep soundly, little Thorlak,
Where all thy peers have lain,
A hero of no battle,

A saint without a stain!

Thy courage be upon thee,
Unblemished by regret,
For that adventure whither
Thy tiny march was set.

The sunshine be above thee,
With birds and winds and trees.
Thy way-fellows inherit
No better things than these.

And silence be about thee,
Turned back from this our war
To front alone the valley
Of night without a star.

The soul of love and valor,
Indifferent to fame,
Be with thee, heart of vikings,
Beyond the breath of blame.

Thy moiety of manhood
Unspent and fair, go down,
And, unabashed, encounter
Thy brothers of renown.

So modest in thy freehold
And tenure of the earth,
Thy needs, for all our meddling,
Are few and little worth.

Content thee, not with pity;
Be solaced, not with tears;
But when the whitethroats waken
Through the revolving years,

Hereafter be that peerless
And dirging cadence, child,
Thy threnody unsullied,
Melodious, and wild.

Then winter be thy housing,
Thy lullaby the rain,
Thou hero of no battle,
Thou saint without a stain.

In the warm blue heart of the hills
My beautiful, beautiful one
Sleeps where he laid him down
Before the journey was done.

All the long summer day
The ghosts of noon draw nigh,
And the tremulous aspens hear
The footing of winds go by.

Down to the gates of the sea,
Out of the gates of the west,
Journeys the whispering river
Before the place of his rest.

The road he loved to follow
When June came by his door,
Out through the dim blue haze
Leads, but allures no more.

The trailing shadows of clouds
Steal from the slopes and are gone;
The myriad life in the grass
Stirs, but he slumbers on;

The inland wandering tern
Skreel as they forage and fly;
His loons on the lonely reach
Utter their querulous cry;

Over the floating lilies
A dragon-fly tacks and steers;
Far in the depth of the blue
A martin settles and veers;

To every roadside thistle
A gold-brown butterfly clings;
But he no more companions
All the dear vagrant things.

The strong red journeying sun,
The pale and wandering rain,
Will roam on the hills forever
And find him never again.

Then twilight falls with the touch
Of a hand that soothes and stills,
And a swamp-robin sings into light
The lone white star of the hills.

Alone in the dusk he sings,
And a burden of sorrow and wrong
Is lifted up from the earth
And carried away in his song.

Alone in the dusk he sings,
And the joy of another day
Is folded in peace and borne
On the drift of years away.

But there in the heart of the hills
My beautiful weary one
Sleeps where he laid him down;
And the large sweet night is begun.

AN AFTERWORD

To G. B. R.

Brother, the world above you
Is very fair to-day,
And all things seem to love you
The old accustomed way.

Here in the heavenly weather
In June's white arms you sleep,
Where once on the hills together
Your haunts you used to keep.

The idling sun that lazes
Along the open field
And gossips to the daisies
Of secrets unrevealed;

The wind that stirs the grasses
A moment, and then stills
Their trouble as he passes
Up to the darkling hills, —

And to the breezy clover
Has many things to say

Of that unwearied rover
Who once went by this way;

The miles of elm-treed meadows;
The clouds that voyage on,
Streeling their noiseless shadows
From countries of the sun;

The tranquil river reaches
And the pale stars of dawn;
The thrushes in their beeches
For reverie withdrawn;

With all your forest fellows
In whom the blind heart calls,
For whom the green leaf yellows,
On whom the red leaf falls;

The dumb and tiny creatures
Of flower and blade and sod,
That dimly wear the features
And attributes of God;

The airy migrant comers
On gauzy wings of fire,
Those wanderers and roamers
Of indefinite desire;

The rainbirds and all dwellers
In solitude and peace,
Those lingerers and foretellers
Of infinite release;

Yea, all the dear things living
That rove or bask or swim,
Remembering and misgiving,
Have felt the day grow dim.

Even the glad things growing,
Blossom and fruit and stem,
Are poorer for your going
Because you were of them.

Yet since you loved to cherish
Their pleading beauty here,
Your heart shall not quite perish
In all the golden year;

But God's great dream above them
Must be a tinge less pale,
Because you lived to love them
And make their joy prevail.

SEVEN WIND SONGS

Now these are the seven wind songs
For Andrew Straton's death,
Blown through the reeds of the river,
A sigh of the world's last breath,

Where the flickering red auroras
Out on the dark sweet hills
Follow all night through the forest
The cry of the whip-poor-wills.

For the meanings of life are many,
But the purpose of love is one,
Journeying, tarrying, lonely
As the sea wind or the sun.

I

Wind of the Northern land,
Wind of the sea,
No more his dearest hand
Comes back to me.

Wind of the Northern gloom,
Wind of the sea,
Wandering waifs of doom
Feckless are we.

Wind of the Northern land,
Wind of the sea,
I cannot understand
How these things be.

II

Wind of the low red morn
At the world's end,
Over the standing corn

Whisper and bend.

Then through the low red morn
At the world's end,
Far out from sorrow's bourne,
Down glory's trend,

Tell the last years forlorn
At the world's end,
Of my one peerless born
Comrade and friend.

III

Wind of the April stars,
Wind of the dawn,
Whether God nears or fars,
He lived and shone.

Wind of the April night,
Wind of the dawn,
No more my heart's delight
Bugles me on.

Wind of the April rain,
Wind of the dawn,
Lull the old world from pain
Till pain be gone.

IV

Wind of the summer noon,
Wind of the hills,
Gently the hand of June
Stays thee and stills.

Far off, untouched by tears,
Raptures or ills,
Sleeps he a thousand years
Out on the hills.

Wind of the summer noon,
Wind of the hills,
Is the land fair and boon
Whither he wills?

Wind of the gulfs of night,
Wind of the sea,
Where the pale streamers light
My world for me,—

Breath of the wintry Norns,
Frost-touch or sleep,—
He whom my spirit mourns
Deep beyond deep

To the last void and dim
Where ages stream—
Is there no room for him
In all this dream?

Wind of the outer waste,
Threne of the outer world,
Leash of the stars unlaced,
Morning unfurled,

Somewhere at God's great need,
I know not how,
With the old strength and speed
He is come now;

Therefore my soul is glad
With the old pride,
Tho' this small life is sad
Here in my side.

Wind of the driven snow,
Wind of the sea,
On a long trail and slow
Farers are we.

Wind of the Northern gloom,
Wind of the sea,
Shall I one day resume
His love for me?

Wind of the driven snow,
Wind of the sea,
Then shall thy vagrant know
How these things be.

These are the seven wind songs
For Andrew Straton's rest,
From the hills of the Scarlet Hunter
And the trail of the endless quest.

The wells of the sunrise harken,
They wait for a year and a day:
Only the calm sure thrushes
Fluting the world away!

For the husk of life is sorrow;
But the kernels of joy remain,
Teeming and blind and eternal
As the hill wind or the rain.

ANDREW STRATON

Andrew Straton was my friend,
With his Saxon eyes and hair,
And his loyal viking spirit,
Like an islesman of the North
With his earldom on the sea.

At his birth the mighty Mother
Made of him a fondling one,
Hushed from pain within her arms,
With her seal upon his lips;

And from that day he was numbered
With the sons of consolation,
Peace and cheer were in his hands,
And her secret in his will.

Now the night has Andrew Straton
Housed from wind and storm forever
In a chamber of the gloom
Where no window fronts the morning,
Lulled to rest at last from roving
To the music of the rain.

And his sleep is in the far-off
Alien villages of the dusk,
Where there is no voice of welcome
To the country of the strangers,
Save the murmur of the pines.

And the fitful winds all day
Through the grass with restless footfalls
Haunt about his narrow door,
Muttering their vast unknown
Border balladry of time,
To the hoarse rote of the sea.

There he reassumes repose,
He who never learned unrest
Here amid our fury of toil,
Undisturbed though all about him
To the cohorts of the night
Sound the bugles of the spring;
And his slumber is not broken
When along the granite hills
Flare the torches of the dawn.

More to me than kith or kin
Was the silence of his speech;
And the quiet of his eyes,
Gathered from the lonely sweep
Of the hyacinthine hills,
Better to the failing spirit
Than a river land in June:
And to look for him at evening
Was more joy than many friends.

As the woodland brooks at noon
Were his brown and gentle hands,
And his face as the hill country
Touched with the red autumn sun

Frank and patient and untroubled
Save by the old trace of doom
In the story of the world.
So the years went brightening by.

Now a lyric wind and weather
Breaks the leaguer of the frost,
And the shining rough month March
Crumbles into sun and rain;
But the glad and murmurous year

Wheels above his rest and wakens
Not a dream for Andrew Straton.

Now the uplands hold an echo
From the meadow lands at morn;
And the marshes hear the rivers
Rouse their giant heart once more,—

Hear the crunching floe start seaward
From a thousand valley floors;
While far on amid the hills
Under stars in the clear night,
The replying, the replying,
Of the ice-cold rivulets
Plashing down the solemn gorges
In their arrowy blue speed,
Fills and frets the crisp blue twilight
With innumerable sound,—
With the whisper of the spring.

But the melting fields are empty,
Something ails the bursting year.

Ah, now helpless, O my rivers,
Are your lifted voices now!
Where is all the sweet compassion
Once your murmur held for me?
Cradled in your dells, I listened
To your crooning, learned your language,
Born your brother and your kin.

When I had the morn for revel,
You made music at my door;
Now the days go darkling on,
And I cannot guess your words.
Shall young joy have troops of neighbors,
While this grief must house alone?

O my brothers of the hills,
Who abide through stress and change,
On the borders of our sorrow,
With no part in human tears,
Lift me up your voice again
And put by this grievous thing!

Ah, my rivers, Andrew Straton
Leaves me here a vacant world!

I must hear the roar of cities
And the jargon of the schools,
With no word of that one spirit
Who was steadfast as the sun
And kept silence with the stars.
I must sit and hear the babble
Of the worldling and the fool,
Prating know-alls and reformers
Busy to improve on man,
With their chatter about God;
Nowhere, nowhere the blue eyes,
With their swift and grave regard,
Falling on me with God's look.

I have seen and known and loved
One who was too sure for sorrow,
Too serenely wise for haste,
Too compassionate for scorn,
Fearless man and faultless comrade,
One great heart whose beat was love.

In a thousand thousand hollows
Of the hills to-day there twinkle
Icy-blue handbreadths of April,
Where the sinking snows decay
In the everlasting sun;
And a thousand tiny creatures
Stretch their heart to fill the world.

Now along the wondrous trail
Andrew Straton loved to follow
Day by day and year on year,
The awaited sure return
Of all sleeping forest things
Is reheralded abroad,
Till the places of their journey,—
Wells the frost no longer hushes,
Ways no drift can bury now,
Wood and stream and road and hillside,—
Hail their coming as of old.

But my beautiful lost comrade
Of the golden heart, whose life
Rang through April like a voice
Through some Norland saga, crying
Skoal to death, comes not again;
Time shall not revive that presence
More desired than all the flowers,

Longer wished for than the birds.

April comes, but April's lover
Is departed and not here.

Sojourning beyond the frost,
He delays; and now no more,—
Though the goldenwings are come
With their resonant tattoo,
And along the barrier pines
Morning reddens on the hills
Where the thrushes wake before it,—
No more to the summoning flutes
Of the forest Andrew Straton
Gets him forth afoot, light-hearted,
On the unfrequented ways
With companionable Spring.

Only the old dreams return.
So I shape me here this fancy,
Foolish me! of Andrew Straton;
How the lands of that new kindred
Have detained him with allegiance,
And some far day I shall find him,
There as here my only captain,
Master of the utmost isles
In the ampler straits of sea.

Out of the blue melting distance
Of the dreamy southward range
Journey back the vagrant winds,
Sure and indolent as time;
And the trembling wakened wood-flowers
Lift their gentle tiny faces
To the sunlight; and the rainbirds
From the lonely cedar barrens
Utter their far pleading cry.

Up across the swales and burnt lands
Where the soft gray tinges purple,
Mouldering into scarlet mist,
Comes the sound as of a marching,
The low murmur of the April
In the many-rivered hills.

Then there stirs the old vague rapture,
Like a wanderer come back,
Still desiring, scathed but deathless,

From beyond the bourne of tears,
Wayworn to his vacant cabin,
To this foolish fearless heart.

Soon the large mild stars of springtime
Will resume the ancient twilight
And restore the heart of earth
To unvexed eternal poise;
For the great Will, calm and lonely,
Can no mortal grief derange,
No lost memories perturb;
And the sluices of the morning
Will be opened, and the daybreak
Well with bird-calls and with brook-notes,
Till there be no more despair
In the gold dream of the world.

THE GRAVE-TREE

Let me have a scarlet maple
For the grave-tree at my head,
With the quiet sun behind it,
In the years when I am dead.

Let me have it for a signal,
Where the long winds stream and stream,
Clear across the dim blue distance,
Like a horn blown in a dream;

Scarlet when the April vanguard
Bugles up the laggard Spring,
Scarlet when the bannered Autumn,
Marches by unwavering.

It will comfort me with honey
When the shining rifts and showers
Sweep across the purple valley
And bring back the forest flowers.

It will be my leafy cabin,
Large enough when June returns
And I hear the golden thrushes
Flute and hesitate by turns.

And in fall, some yellow morning,
When the stealthy frost has come,

Leaf by leaf it will befriend me
As with comrades going home.

Let me have the Silent Valley
And the hill that fronts the east,
So that I can watch the morning
Redden and the stars released.

Leave me in the Great Lone Country,
For I shall not be afraid
With the shy moose and the beaver
There within my scarlet shade.

I would sleep, but not too soundly,
Where the sunning partridge drums,
Till the crickets hush before him
When the Scarlet Hunter comes.

That will be in warm September,
In the stillness of the year,
When the river-blue is deepest
And the other world is near.

When the apples burn their reddest
And the corn is in the sheaves,
I shall stir and waken lightly
At a footfall in the leaves.

It will be the Scarlet Hunter
Come to tell me time is done;
On the idle hills forever
There will stand the idle sun.

There the wind will stay to whisper
Many wonders to the reeds;
But I shall not fear to follow
Where my Scarlet Hunter leads.

I shall know him in the darkling
Murmur of the river bars,
While his feet are on the mountains
Treading out the smoldering stars.

I shall know him, in the sunshine
Sleeping in my scarlet tree,
Long before he halts beside it
Stooping down to summon me.

Then fear not, my friends, to leave me
In the boding autumn vast;
There are many things to think of
When the roving days are past.

Leave me by the scarlet maple,
When the journeying shadows fail,
Waiting till the Scarlet Hunter
Pass upon the endless trail.

Bliss Carman - An Appreciation

How many Canadians—how many even among the few who seek to keep themselves informed of the best in contemporary literature, who are ever on the alert for the new voices—realise, or even suspect, that this Northern land of theirs has produced a poet of whom it may be affirmed with confidence and assurance that he is of the great succession of English poets? Yet such—strange and unbelievable though it may seem—is in very truth the case, that poet being (to give him his full name) William Bliss Carman. Canada has full right to be proud of her poets, a small body though they are; but not only does Mr. Carman stand high and clear above them all—his place (and time cannot but confirm and justify the assertion) is among those men whose poetry is the shining glory of that great English literature which is our common heritage.

If any should ask why, if what has been just said is so, there has been—as must be admitted—no general recognition of the fact in the poet's home land, I would answer that there are various and plausible, if not good, reasons for it.

First of all, the poet, as thousands more of our young men of ambition and confidence have done, went early to the United States, and until recently, except for rare and brief visits to his old home down by the sea, has never returned to Canada—though for all that, I am able to state, on his own authority, he is still a Canadian citizen. Then all his books have had their original publication in the United States, and while a few of them have subsequently carried the imprints of Canadian publishers, none of these can be said ever to have made any special effort to push their sale. Another reason for the fact above mentioned is that Mr. Carman has always scorned to advertise himself, while his work has never been the subject of the log-rolling and booming which the work of many another poet has had—to his ultimate loss. A further reason is that he follows a rule of his own in preparing his books for publication. Most poets publish a volume of their work as soon as, through their industry and perseverance, they have material enough on hand to make publication desirable in their eyes. Not so with Mr. Carman, however, his rule being not to publish until he has done sufficient work of a certain general character or key to make a volume. As a result, you cannot fully know or estimate his work by one book, or two books, or even half a dozen; you must possess or be familiar with every one of the score and more volumes which contain his output of poetry before you can realise how great and how many-sided is his genius.

It is a common remark on the part of those who respond readily to the vigorous work of Kipling, or Masefield, even our own Service, that Bliss Carman's poetry has no relation to or concern with ordinary, everyday life. One would suppose that most persons who cared for poetry at all turned to it as a relief from or counter to the burdens and vexations of the daily round; but in any event, the remark referred to seems to me to indicate either the most casual acquaintance with Mr. Carman's work, or a complete misunderstanding and misapprehension of the meaning of it. I grant that you will find little or nothing in it all to remind you of the grim realities and vexing social problems of this modern existence of ours; but to say or to suggest that these things do not exist for Mr. Carman is to say or to suggest something which is the reverse of true. The truth is, he is aware of them as only one with the sensitive organism of a poet can be; but he does not feel that he has a call or mission to remedy them, and still less to sing of them. He therefore leaves the immediate problems of the day to those who choose, or are led, to occupy themselves therewith, and turns resolutely away to dwell upon those things which for him possess infinitely greater importance.

"What are they?" one who knows Mr. Carman only as, say, a lyrist of spring or as a singer of the delights of vagabondia probably will ask in some wonder. Well, the things which concern him above all, I would answer, are first, and naturally, the beauty and wonder of this world of ours, and next the mystery of the earthly pilgrimage of the human soul out of eternity and back into it again.

The poems in the present volume—which, by the way, can boast the high honor of being the very first regular Canadian edition of his work—will be evidence ample and conclusive to every reader, I am sure, of the place which

The perennial enchanted
Lovely world and all its lore

occupy in the heart and soul of Bliss Carman, as well as of the magical power with which he is able to convey the deep and unfailing satisfaction and delight which they possess for him. They, however, represent his latest period (he has had three well-defined periods), comprising selections from three of his last published volumes: The Rough Rider, Echoes from Vagabondia, and April Airs, together with a number of new poems, and do not show, except here and there and by hints and flashes, how great is his preoccupation with the problem of man's existence—

—the hidden import
Of man's eternal plight.

This is manifest most in certain of his earlier books, for in these he turns and returns to the greatest of all the problems of man almost constantly, probing, with consummate and almost unrivalled use of the art of expression, for the secret which surely, he clearly feels, lies hidden somewhere, to be discovered if one could but pierce deeply enough. Pick up Behind the Arras, and as you turn over page after page you cannot but observe how incessantly the poet's mind—like the minds of his two great masters, Browning and Whitman—works at this problem. In "Behind the Arras," the title poem; "In the Wings," "The Crimson House," "The Lodger," "Beyond the Gamut," "The Juggler"—yes, in every poem in the book—he takes up and handles the strange thing we know as, or call, life, turning it now this way, now that, in an effort to find out its meaning and purpose. He comes but little nearer success in this than do most of the rest of men, of course; but the magical and ever-fresh beauty of his expression, the haunting melody of his lines, the variety of his images and figures and the depth and range of his thought, put his searchings and ponderings in a class by themselves.

Lengthy quotation from Mr. Carman's books is not permitted here, and I must guide myself accordingly, though with reluctance, because I believe that in a study such as this the subject should be allowed to speak for himself as much as possible. In "Behind the Arras" the poet describes the passage from life to death as

A cadence dying down unto its source
In music's course,

and goes on to speak of death as

—the broken rhythm of thought and man,
The sweep and span
Of memory and hope
About the orbit where they still must grope
For wider scope,

To be through thousand springs restored, renewed,
With love imbrued,
With increments of will
Made strong, perceiving unattainment still
From each new skill.

Now follow some verses from "Behind the Gamut," to my mind the poet's greatest single achievement;

As fine sand spread on a disc of silver,
At some chord which bids the motes combine,
Heeding the hidden and reverberant impulse,
Shifts and dances into curve and line,

The round earth, too, haply, like a dust-mote,
Was set whirling her assigned sure way,
Round this little orb of her ecliptic
To some harmony she must obey.

And what of man?

Linked to all his half-accomplished fellows,
Through unfrontiered provinces to range—
Man is but the morning dream of nature,
Roused to some wild cadence weird and strange.

Here, now, are some verses from "Pulvis et Umbra," which is to be found in Mr. Carman's first book, Low Tide on Grand Pré, and in which the poet addresses a moth which a storm has blown into his window:

For man walks the world with mourning
Down to death and leaves no trace,
With the dust upon his forehead,
And the shadow on his face.

Pillared dust and fleeing shadow

As the roadside wind goes by,
And the fourscore years that vanish
In the twinkling of an eye.

"Pillared dust and fleeing shadow." Where in all our English literature will one find the life history of man summed up more briefly and, at the same time, more beautifully, than in that wonderful line? Now follows a companion verse to those just quoted, taken from "Lord of My Heart's Elation," which stands in the forefront of From the Green Book of the Bards. It may be remarked here that while the poet recurs again and again to some favorite thought or idea, it is never in the same words. His expression is always new and fresh, showing how deep and true is his inspiration. Again it is man who is pictured:

A fleet and shadowy column
Of dust and mountain rain,
To walk the earth a moment
And be dissolved again.

But while Mr. Carman's speculations upon life's meaning and the mystery of the future cannot but appeal to the thoughtful-minded, it is as an interpreter of nature that he makes his widest appeal. Bliss Carman, I must say here, and emphatically, is no mere landscape-painter; he never, or scarcely ever, paints a picture of nature for its own sake. He goes beyond the outward aspect of things and interprets or translates for us with less keen senses as only a poet whose feeling for nature is of the deepest and profoundest, who has gone to her whole-heartedly and been taken close to her warm bosom, can do. Is this not evident from these verses from "The Great Return"—originally called "The Pagan's Prayer," and for some inscrutable reason to be found only in the limited Collected Poems, issued in two stately volumes in 1905.

When I have lifted up my heart to thee,
Thou hast ever hearkened and drawn near,
And bowed thy shining face close over me,
Till I could hear thee as the hill-flowers hear.

When I have cried to thee in lonely need,
Being but a child of thine bereft and wrung,
Then all the rivers in the hills gave heed;
And the great hill-winds in thy holy tongue—

That ancient incommunicable speech—
The April stars and autumn sunsets know—
Soothed me and calmed with solace beyond reach
Of human ken, mysterious and low.

Who can read or listen to those moving lines without feeling that Mr. Carman is in very truth a poet of nature—nay, Nature's own poet? But how could he be other when, in "The Breath of the Reed" (From the Green Book of the Bards), he makes the appeal?

Make me thy priest, O Mother,
And prophet of thy mood,
With all the forest wonder

Enraptured and imbued.

As becomes such a poet, and particularly a poet whose birth-month is April, Mr. Carman sings much of the early spring. Again and again he takes up his woodland pipe, and lo! Pan himself and all his train troop joyously before us. Yet the singer's notes for all his singing never become wearied or strident; his airs are ever new and fresh; his latest songs are no less spontaneous and winning than were his first, written how many years ago, while at the same time they have gained in beauty and melody. What heart will not stir to the vibrant music of his immortal "Spring Song," which was originally published in the first Songs from Vagabondia, and the opening verses of which follow?

Make me over, mother April,
When the sap begins to stir!
When thy flowery hand delivers
All the mountain-prisoned rivers,
And thy great heart beats and quivers
To revive the days that were,
Make me over, mother April,
When the sap begins to stir!

Take my dust and all my dreaming,
Count my heart-beats one by one,
Send them where the winters perish;
Then some golden noon recherish
And restore them in the sun,
Flower and scent and dust and dreaming,
With their heart-beats every one!

That poem is sufficient in itself to prove that Bliss Carman has full right and title to be called Spring's own lyrist, though it may be remarked here that not all his spring poems are so unfeignedly joyous. Many of them indeed, have a touch, or more than a touch, of wistfulness, for the poet knows well that sorrow lurks under all joy, deep and well hidden though it may be.

Mr. Carman sings equally finely, though perhaps not so frequently, of summer and the other seasons; but as he has other claims upon our attention, I shall forbear to labor the fact, particularly as the following collection demonstrates it sufficiently. One of those other claims is as a writer of sea poetry. Few poets, it may be said, have pictured the majesty and the mystery, the beauty and the terror of the sea, better than he. His Ballads of Lost Haven is a veritable treasure-house for those whose spirits find kinship in wide expanses of moving waters. One of the best known poems in this volume is "The Gravedigger," which opens thus:

Oh, the shambling sea is a sexton old,
And well his work is done.
With an equal grave for lord and knave,
He buries them every one.

Then hoy and rip, with a rolling hip,
He makes for the nearest shore;
And God, who sent him a thousand ship,

Will send him a thousand more;
But some he'll save for a bleaching grave,
And shoulder them in to shore—
Shoulder them in, shoulder them in,
Shoulder them in to shore.

In "The City of the Sea" (Last Songs from Vagabondia) Mr. Carman speaks of the seabells sounding

The eternal cadence of sea sorrow
For Man's lot and immemorial wrong—
The lost strains that haunt the human dwelling
With the ghost of song.

Elsewhere he speaks of

The great sea, mystic and musical.

And here from another poem is a striking picture:

... the old sea
Seems to whimper and deplore
Mourning like a childless crone
With her sorrow left alone—
The eternal human cry
To the heedless passer-by.

I have said above that Mr. Carman has had three distinct periods, and intimated that the poems in the following collection are of his third period. The first period may be said to be represented by the Low Tide and Behind the Arras volumes, while the second is displayed in the three volumes of Songs from Vagabondia, which he published in association with his friend Richard Hovey. Bliss Carman was from the first too original and individual a poet to be directly influenced by anyone else; but there can be no doubt that his friendship with Hovey helped to turn him from over-preoccupation with mysteries which, for all their greatness, are not for man to solve, to an intenser realisation of the beauty and loveliness of the world about him and of the joys of human fellowship. The result is seen in such poems as "Spring Song," quoted in part above, and his perhaps equally well-known "The Joys of the Road," which appeared in the same volume with that poem, and a few verses from which follow:

Now the joys of the road are chiefly these:
A crimson touch on the hardwood trees;

A vagrant's morning wide and blue,
In early fall, when the wind walks, too;

A shadowy highway cool and brown,
Alluring up and enticing down

From rippled waters and dappled swamp,
From purple glory to scarlet pomp;

The outward eye, the quiet will,
And the striding heart from hill to hill.

Some of the finest of arman's work is contained in his elegiac or memorial poems, in which he commemorates Keats, Shelley, William Blake, Lincoln, Stevenson, and other men for whom he has a kindred feeling, and also friends whom he has loved and lost. Listen to these moving lines from "Non Omnis Moriar," written in memory of Gleeson White, and to be found in Last Songs from Vagabondia:

There is a part of me that knows,
Beneath incertitude and fear,
I shall not perish when I pass
Beyond mortality's frontier;

But greatly having joyed and grieved,
Greatly content, shall hear the sigh
Of the strange wind across the lone
Bright lands of taciturnity.

In patience therefore I await
My friend's unchanged benign regard,—
Some April when I too shall be
Spilt water from a broken shard.

In "The White Gull," written for the centenary of the birth of Shelley in 1892, and included in By the Aurelian Wall, he thus apostrophizes that clear and shining spirit:

O captain of the rebel host,
Lead forth and far!
Thy toiling troopers of the night
Press on the unavailing fight;
The sombre field is not yet lost,
With thee for star.

Thy lips have set the hail and haste
Of clarions free
To bugle down the wintry verge
Of time forever, where the surge
Thunders and trembles on a waste
And open sea.

In "A Seamark," a threnody for Robert Louis Stevenson, which appears in the same volume, the poet hails "R.L.S." (of whose tribe he may be said to be truly one) as

The master of the roving kind,

and goes on:

O all you hearts about the world
In whom the truant gypsy blood,
Under the frost of this pale time,
Sleeps like the daring sap and flood
That dreams of April and reprieve!
You whom the haunted vision drives,
Incredulous of home and ease.
Perfection's lovers all your lives!

You whom the wander-spirit loves
To lead by some forgotten clue
Forever vanishing beyond
Horizon brinks forever new;
Our restless loved adventurer,
On secret orders come to him,
Has slipped his cable, cleared the reef,
And melted on the white sea-rim.

"Perfection's lovers all your lives." Of these, it may be said without qualification, is Bliss Carman himself.

No summary of Mr. Carman's work, however cursory, would be worthy of the name if it omitted mention of his ventures in the realm of Greek myth. From the Book of Myths is made up of work of that sort, every poem in it being full of the beauty of phrase and melody of which Mr. Carman alone has the secret. The finest poems in the book, barring the opening one, "Overlord," are "Daphne," "The Dead Faun," "Hylas," and "At Phædra's Tomb," but I can do no more here than name them, for extracts would fail to reveal their full beauty. And beauty, after all is said, is the first and last thing with Mr. Carman. As he says himself somewhere:

The joy of the hand that hews for beauty
Is the dearest solace under the sun.

And again

The eternal slaves of beauty
Are the masters of the world.

A slave—a happy, willing slave—to beauty is the poet himself, and the world can never repay him for the message of beauty which he has brought it.

Kindred to From the Book of Myths, but much more important, is Sappho: One Hundred Lyrics, one of the most successful of the numerous attempts which have been made to recapture the poems by that high priestess of song which remain to us only in fragments. Mr. Carman, as Charles G. D. Roberts points out in an introduction to the volume, has made no attempt here at translation or paraphrasing; his venture has been "the most perilous and most alluring in the whole field of poetry"—that of imaginative and, at the same time, interpretive construction. Brief quotation again would fail to convey an adequate idea of the exquisiteness of the work, and all I can do, therefore, is to urge all lovers of real poetry to possess themselves of Sappho: One Hundred Lyrics, for it is literally a storehouse of lyric beauty.

I must not fail here to speak of From the Book of Valentines, which contains some lovely things, notably "At the Great Release." This is not only one of the finest of all Mr. Carman's poems, but it is also one of the finest poems of our time. It is a love poem, and no one possessing any real feeling for poetry can read it without experiencing that strange thrill of the spirit which only the highest form of poetry can communicate. "Morning and Evening," "In an Iris Meadow," and "A letter from Lesbos" must be also mentioned. In the last named poem, Sappho is represented as writing to Gorgo, and expresses herself in these moving words:

If the high gods in that triumphant time
Have calendared no day for thee to come
Light-hearted to this doorway as of old,
Unmoved I shall behold their pomps go by—
The painted seasons in their pageantry,
The silvery progressions of the moon,
And all their infinite ardors unsubdued,
Pass with the wind replenishing the earth

Incredulous forever I must live
And, once thy lover, without joy behold,
The gradual uncounted years go by,
Sharing the bitterness of all things made.

Mention must be now made of Songs of the Sea Children, which can be described only as a collection of the sweetest and tenderest love lyrics written in our time—

—the lyric songs
The earthborn children sing,
When wild-wood laughter throngs
The shy bird-throats of spring;
When there's not a joy of the heart
But flies like a flag unfurled,
And the swelling buds bring back
The April of the world.

So perfect and complete are these lyrics that it would be almost sacrilege to quote any of them unless entire. Listen however, to these verses:

The day is lost without thee,
The night has not a star.
Thy going is an empty room
Whose door is left ajar.

Depart: it is the footfall
Of twilight on the hills.
Return: and every rood of ground
Breaks into daffodils.

There are those who will have it that Bliss Carman has been away from Canada so long that he has ceased to be, in a real sense, a Canadian. Such assume rather than know, for a very little study of his work would show them that it is shot through and through with the poet's feeling for the land of his birth. Memories of his childhood and youthful years down by the sea are still fresh in Mr. Carman's mind, and inspire him again and again in his writing. "A Remembrance," at the beginning of the present collection, may be pointed to as a striking instance of this, but proof positive is the volume, Songs from a Northern Garden, for it could have been written only by a Canadian, born and bred, one whose heart and soul thrill to the thought of Canada. I would single out from this volume for special mention as being "Canadian" in the fullest sense "In a Grand Pré Garden," "The Keeper's Silence," "At Home and Abroad," "Killoleet," and "Above the Gaspereau," but have no space to quote from them.

But Mr. Carman is not only a Canadian, he is also a Briton; and evidence of this is his Ode on the Coronation, written on the occasion of the crowning of King Edward VII in 1902. This poem—the very existence of which is hardly known among us—ought to be put in the hands of every child and youth who speaks the English tongue, for no other, I dare maintain—nothing by Kipling, or Newbolt, or any other of our so-called "Imperial singers"—expresses more truly and more movingly the deep feeling of love and reverence which the very thought of England evokes in every son of hers, even though it may never have been his to see her white cliffs rise or to tread her storied ground:

O England, little mother by the sleepless Northern tide,
Having bred so many nations to devotion, trust, and pride,
Very tenderly we turn
With welling hearts that yearn
Still to love you and defend you,—let the sons of men discern
Wherein your right and title, might and majesty, reside.

In concluding this, I greatly fear, lamentably inadequate study, I come to the collection which follows, and which, as intimated above, represents the work of Mr. Carman's latest period. I must say at once that, while I yield to no one in admiration for Low Tide and the other books of that period, or for the work of the second period, as represented by the Songs from Vagabondia volumes, I have no hesitation in declaring that I regard the poet's work of the past few years with even higher admiration. It may not possess the force and vigor of the work which preceded it; but anything seemingly missing in that respect is more than made up for me by increased beauty and clarity of expression. The mysticism—verging, or more than verging, at times on symbolism—which marked his earlier poems, and which hung, as it were, as a veil between them and the reader, has gone, and the poet's thought or theme now lies clearly before us as in a mirror. What—to take a verse from the following pages at random—could be more pellucid, more crystal clear in expression—what indeed, could come closer to that achieving of the impossible at which every real poet must aim—than this from "In Gold Lacquer".

Gold are the great trees overhead,
And gold the leaf-strewn grass,
As though a cloth of gold were spread
To let a seraph pass.
And where the pageant should go by,
Meadow and wood and stream,
The world is all of lacquered gold,
Expectant as a dream.

The poet, happily, has fully recovered from the serious illness which laid him low some two years ago, and which for a time caused his friends and admirers the gravest concern, and so we may look forward hopefully to seeing further volumes of verse come from the press to make certain his name and fame. But if, for any reason, this should not be—which the gods forfend!—Later Poems, I dare affirm, must and will be regarded as the fine flower and crowning achievement of the genius and art of Bliss Carman.

R. H. HATHAWAY.
Toronto, 1921.

Bliss Carman – A Short Biography

William Bliss Carman was born in Fredericton, in New Brunswick on April 15th 1861. 'Bliss' was his mother's maiden name. She was descended from Daniel Bliss of Concord, Massachusetts, who was the great-grandfather to Ralph Waldo Emerson.

Carman was educated at Fredericton Collegiate School. Here, under the influence of the headmaster George Robert Parkin, he gained an appreciation of classical literature and was introduced to the poetry of many of the Pre-Raphaelites especially Dante Gabriel Rossetti and Algernon Charles Swinburne.

From here he graduated to the University of New Brunswick, obtaining his B.A. there in 1881. As is common with so many writers his first published piece was for the University magazine and for Carman that was in 1879.

England now beckoned and he spent a year at Oxford and then the University of Edinburgh (1882–1883). He returned home to Canada to work on his M.A. which he obtained from the University of New Brunswick in 1884.

Tragically his father died in January, 1885, followed by his mother in February of the following year. Carman now enrolled in Harvard University for a year. There he met and was part of a literary circle that included the American poet Richard Hovey, who would become his close friend, and later collaborator, on the successful Vagabondia poetry series. Carman and Hovey were members of the "Visionists" circle along with Herbert Copeland and F. Holland Day, who would later form the Boston publishing firm Copeland & Day and, in turn, launch Vagabondia.

After Harvard Carman briefly returned to Canada, but was back in Boston by February of 1890 saying "Boston is one of the few places where my critical education and tastes could be of any use to me in earning money. New York and London are about the only other places." However, he was unable to find work in Boston but was more successful in New York becoming the literary editor of the semi-religious New York Independent. There he helped Canadian poets get published and introduced them to a wider readership than they could receive in Canada.

However, Carman and work as an editor were not destined for a long career together and he was dismissed in 1892. There followed short stays with Current Literature, Cosmopolitan, The Chap-Book, and The Atlantic Monthly. Whilst these appointments provided the basis for a career and an income he was not suited to their demands. From 1895 he would only work as a contributor to magazines and newspapers whilst he worked on his volumes of poetry.

Carman first published a book of poetry in 1893 with Low Tide on Grand Pré. He had written the title poem in the summer of 1886 and it had (whilst he was still at Harvard) been published in the spring of 1887 by Atlantic Monthly. Despite its critical acceptance there was no Canadian company prepared to publish the volume. When an American company did so it went bankrupt. Life was becoming difficult for the young poet.

The following year was decidedly better. His partnership with Richard Hovey had given birth to Songs of Vagabondia and it was published by their friends at Copeland & Day. It was an immediate success. The young men were delighted at such a reception. It quickly sold out and was re-printed a number of times. Although these re-prints were small (usually 500-1000 copies) they were frequent.

On the back of this success they would write a further three volumes, which in their turn were almost as successful. They quickly became the center of a cult following, especially among students who empathized with the poetry's anti-materialistic themes, its celebration of personal freedom, and its glorification of comradeship."

The success of Songs of Vagabondia prompted the Boston firm, Stone & Kimball, to reissue Low Tide on Grand Pré and to hire Carman as the editor of its literary journal, The Chapbook. This ceased after a year when the company relocated and Carman expressed his desire to remain in Boston.

In 1885 Carman brought out Behind the Arras, a somewhat more serious and philosophical work centered on the premise of a long meditation using the speaker's house and its many rooms as a symbol of life and the choices to be made. However, the idea and its execution did not quite meld.

Signficantly, in 1896, Carman met Mrs Mary Perry King, who rapidly became patron, adviser and sometime lover. She put money in his pocket, and food in his mouth and, when he struck bottom, often repaired his confidence as well as helping to sell the work. She also later became his writing collaborator on two verse dramas.

Mitchell Kennerley, Carman's roommate wrote that, "On the rare occasions they had intimate relations they always advised me of by leaving a bunch of violets — Mary favorite flower — on the pillow of my bed." If her husband, Dr. King, knew of this arrangement he seems not to have objected. He was a great supporter of Carman's career and seemingly his wife's complicated involvement with that.

In 1897 Carman published Ballad of Lost Haven, a collection of poetry about the sea. Its notable poems include the macabre sea shanty, The Gravedigger. The following year, 1898, came By the Aurelian Wall, the title poem itself was an elegy to John Keats and the book a collection of formal elegies.

In 1899 his publisher, Lamson, Wolffe was taken over by the Boston firm of Small, Maynard & Co., who had also acquired the rights to Low Tide on Grand Pré. The copyrights to of his books were now held by one publisher and, in lieu of earnings, Carman took what would ultimately be a disastrous financial stake in the company.

As the century turned Carman was hard at work on what would eventually be a five-volume set of poetry; "Pans Pipes". Pan, the goat-god, was traditionally associated with poetry and the coming together of the earthly and the divine. The five volumes were all published between 1902 – 1905.

The inspiration for this came from Mary who had persuaded Carman to write in both prose and poetry about the ideas of 'unitrinianism.' This drew on the theories of François-Alexandre-Nicolas-Chéri Delsarte and was defined as a strategy of mind-body-spirit harmonization aimed at undoing the physical, psychological, and spiritual damage caused by urban modernity. The definition may be rather woolly but for Carman it resulted in some very fine work across the five-volume series. This shared belief between Mary and Carman created a further bond but did isolate him from his circle of friends.

The excellence of a number of these poems did much to install Carman as the most noted of Canadian Poets and eventually their own Poet Laureate. Among the most often quoted and printed are "The Dead Faun" (from Volume I), "Lord of My Heart's Elation" (Volume II) and many of the erotic poems from Volume III.

In the middle of publication in 1903, Small, Maynard failed and with it went all the assets Carman had tied up in the company.

Carman immediately signed with another Boston publisher, L.C. Page, who would publish seven new books of Carman poetry in this hectic period up to 1905. They released a further three books based on Carman's Transcript columns, and a prose work on Unitrinianism, The Making of Personality, that he'd written with Mary King.

Carman now felt secure enough to pursue his 'dream project,' namely a deluxe edition of his collected poetry to 1903. Page acquired the distribution rights on the condition that the book be sold privately, by subscription. Unfortunately, the demand wasn't there and it failed. Carman was deeply disappointed and lost faith in Page. However, their grip on his copyrights was absolute and sadly no further collected editions were to be published during his lifetime.

By 1904 his income was restricted and the offer to be editor-in-chief of the 10-volume project, The World's Best Poetry, was eagerly accepted.

For Carman perhaps his best years as a poet were now behind him. From 1908 he lived near the Kings' New Canaan, Connecticut, estate, that he named "Sunshine", or in the summer in a cabin in the Catskills, which he called "Moonshine."

With Literary tastes now moving away from what he could provide his income further dwindled and his health started to deteriorate.

In 1912 Carman published the final work in the Vagabondia series. Richard Hovey had died in 1900 and so this last work was purely his. It has a distinct elegiac tone as if remembering the past works themselves.

Although Carman was not politically active he did campaign during the World War One, as a member of the Vigilantes, who supported the American entry into the titanic struggle on the Allied side.

By 1920, Carman was impoverished and recovering from a near-fatal attack of tuberculosis. He returned to Canada and began to undertake a series of publicly successful and somewhat lucrative reading tours, saying "there is nothing worth talking of in book sales compared with reading. Breathless attention, crowded halls, and a strange, profound enthusiasm such as I never guessed could be,' he reported to a friend. 'And good thrifty money too. Think of it! An entirely new life for me, and I am the most surprised person in Canada.'"

On October 28th, 1921 Carman was honored at a dinner held by the newly-formed Canadian Authors' Association, at the Ritz Carlton Hotel in Montreal, where he was crowned Canada's Poet Laureate with a wreath of maple leaves.

Carman is placed among the Confederation Poets, a group that included his cousin, Charles G.D. Roberts, Archibald Lampman, and Duncan Campbell Scott. Carman was perhaps the best and is credited with the widest recognition. However, whilst the others carefully supplemented their income with writing novels and works for the magazines, or even other careers, Carman only wrote poetry together with a small amount of writing on literary ideas, philosophy, and aesthetics.

He continued his reading tours, and by 1925 had finally secured a new Canadian publisher; McClelland & Stewart (Toronto), who issued a collection of selected earlier verse and would now became his main publisher. Although they benefited from Carman's increased popularity and his revered position in Canadian literature, his former publisher L.C. Page would not relinquish its copyrights to his earlier works.

In his last years, Carman was a member of the Halifax literary and social set, The Song Fishermen and in 1927 he edited The Oxford Book of American Verse.

William Bliss Carman died of a brain hemorrhage, at the age of 68, in New Canaan on the 8th June, 1929. He was cremated in New Canaan and his ashes interred at Forest Hill Cemetery, Fredericton, with a national memorial service held at the Anglican cathedral there.

It was only a quarter of a century later, on May 13th, 1954, that a scarlet maple tree was planted at his graveside, to honour his request in the 1892 poem "The Grave-Tree":

Let me have a scarlet maple
For the grave-tree at my head,
With the quiet sun behind it,
In the years when I am dead.

Bliss Carman – A Concise Bibliography

Poetry Collections
Low Tide on Grand Pre: A Book of Lyrics (1893)
Songs from Vagabondia (1894)
A Seamark: A Threnody for Robert Louis Stevenson (1895)
Behind the Arras: A Book of the Unseen (1895)
More Songs from Vagabondia (1896)
Ballads of Lost Haven: A Book of the Sea (1897)
By the Aurelian Wall: And Other Elegies (1898)
A Winter Holiday (1899)
Last Songs from Vagabondia (1901)

Ballads and Lyrics (1902)
Ode on the Coronation of King Edward (1902)
Pipes of Pan: From the Book of Myths (1902)
Pipes of Pan: From the Green Book of the Bards (1903)
Pipes of Pan: Songs of the Sea Children (1904)
Pipes of Pan: Songs from a Northern Garden (1904)
Pipes of Pan: From the Book of Valentines (1905)
Sappho: One Hundred Lyrics (1904)
Poems (1905)
The Rough Rider: And Other Poems (1909)
A Painter's Holiday, and Other Poems (1911)
Echoes from Vagabondia (1912)
April Airs: A Book of New England Lyrics (1916)
The Man of The Marne: And Other Poems (1918)
The Vengeance of Noel Brassard: A Tale of the Acadian Expulsion (1919)
Far Horizons (1925)
Later Poems (1926)
Sanctuary: Sunshine House Sonnets (1929)
Wild Garden (1929)
Bliss Carman's Poems (1931)

Drama

Bliss Carman & Mary Perry King. Daughters of Dawn: A Lyrical Pageant of a Series of Historical Scenes for Presentation with Music and Dancing (1913)
Bliss Carman & Mary Perry King. Earth Deities: And Other Rhythmic Masques (1914)

Prose Collections
The Kinship of Nature (1904)
The Poetry of Life (1905)
The Friendship of Art (1908)
The Making of Personality (1908)
Talks on Poetry and Life; Being a Series of Five Lectures Delivered Before the University of Toronto, December 1925 (Speech). transcribed by Blanche Hume. 1926.
Bliss Carman's Scrap-Book: A Table of Contents (Pierce, Lorne, editor) (1931)

Editor
The World's Best Poetry (10 volumes) (1904)
The Oxford Book of American Verse (U.S. editor) (1927)
Carman, Bliss; Pierce, Lorne, editors (1935). Our Canadian Literature: Representative Verse, English and French.

www.ingramcontent.com/pod-product-compliance
Lightning Source LLC
Chambersburg PA
CBHW060055050426
42448CB00011B/2470